Pocket Poetry Mini-Books

12 Absolutely Adorable Literacy-Building Mini-Books on Favorite Themes for Kids to Read Again and Again—in School or at Home

BY BETSY FRANCO

S C H O L A S T I C
PROFESSIONAL BOOKS

New York • Toronto • London • Auckland • Sydney • Mexico City
New Delhi • Hong Kong • Buenos Aires

For Sarah

Special thanks to Marcy Black, Stephanie Calmenson, Joan Cottle,
Joy N. Hulme, Bobbi Katz, Monica Kulling, Sandra Liatsos,
Katie McAllaster Weaver, Kris Aro McLeod, Marisa Montes,
Leslie Danford Perkins, Lawrence Schimel, Robert Scotellaro,
Jacqueline Sweeney, JoAnne Wetzel, Sarah Wilson, Anita Wintz,
and Caryn Yacowitz who helped make this collection come alive.
I am also very grateful for my wonderful editor for her haiku
and for her ideas and support.

Permissions Information

Marcy Black. "The Garbage Dump" by Marcy Black. Copyright 2001 by Marcy Black. Used by permission of Marian Reiner for the author.

Stephanie Calmenson. Untitled poem which begins "Slither, slither" by Stephanie Calmenson. Copyright 2001 by Stephanie Calmenson. Used by permission of Marian Reiner for the author.

Liza Charlesworth. "Wind" by Liza Charlesworth. Copyright 2001 by Liza Charlesworth. Used by permission of the author.

Marchette Chute. "Crayons" from *Rhymes About Us* by Marchette Chute. Copyright 1974 by E.P. Dutton. Reprinted by permission of Elizabeth Hauser.

Joan Cottle. "Halloween Night" by Joan Cottle. Copyright 2001 by Joan Cottle. Reprinted by permission of Curtis Brown, Ltd.

Aileen Fisher. "On Halloween" from *Out in the Dark and Daylight* by Aileen Fisher. Copyright 1980 by Aileen Fisher. First appeared in *Weekly Reader*. Used by permission of Marian Reiner for the author.

Langston Hughes. "Winter Sweetness" from *The Collected Poems of Langston Hughes*. Used by permission of Alfred A. Knopf, a division of Random House, Inc.

Joy N. Hulme. "Elephant" from What If? Published by Boyds Mills Press. Copyright 1993 Joy N. Hulme. Used by permission of the author. "I'm a Ghost" by Joy N. Hulme is used by permission of the author who controls all rights.

Monica Kulling "Ice Bird" by Monica Kulling. Copyright 2001 by Monica Kulling. Used by permission of the author.

Kris Aro McLeod. "Painting a Summer Day," "The Hundredth Day," and "I'm cold and creamy..." by Kris Aro McLeod. Used by permission of the author.

Marisa Montes. "Rainbow" by Marisa Montes. Copyright 2001 by Marisa Montes. Used by permission of the author.

Leslie Danford Perkins. "Rhinocerecess" by Leslie Danford Perkins. Used by permission of the author who controls all rights.

Lawrence Schimel. "Spider" by Lawrence Schimel. Copyright 2001 by Lawrence Schimel. Used by permission of the author.

Robert Scotellaro. "My Little Brother's Birthday" and "Little Monster's Lullaby" are used by permission of the author who controls all rights.

Jacqueline Sweeney. "Edible" from Quick Poetry Activities (Scholastic Professional Books). Copyright 1994 by Jacqueline Sweeney. Reprinted by permission of Marian Reiner for the author.

Kate McAllaster Weaver. "Rain Cloud" is used by permission of the author who controls all rights.

JoAnne Wetzel. "Train Tracks" by JoAnne Wetzel is used by permission of the author who controls all rights.

Sarah Wilson. "June is a bumble...." From the book *June is a Tune That Jumps On a Stair* (Simon & Schuster, 1992). Copyright 1992 by Sarah Wilson. Used by permission of the author.

Anita Wintz. "Blow and I'll Grow" by Anita Wintz is copyright 2001 by Anita Wintz. "Autographing Winter" by Anita Wintz. Copyright 1999 by Anita Wintz. Both are used by permission of Marian Reiner for the author.

Caryn Yacowitz. "Tell a butterfly..." is used by permission of the author who controls all rights.

Sandra Liatsos. "On the School Bus" and "In the School Room" by Sandra Liatsos are copyright 2001 by Sandra Liatsos. "Sailing With Whales" by Sandra Liatsos is copyright 1991 by Sandra Liatsos and first appeared in Ranger Rick Magazine. All are used by permission of Marian Reiner for the author.

Cover design by **Josué Castilleja**
Cover and interior artwork by **Paige Billin-Frye**
Interior design by **BHG Graphic Designs**

ISBN: 0-439-27859-7
Copyright © 2002 by **Betsy Franco**
All rights reserved.
Printed in the U.S.A.

Contents

The Mini-Books

Introduction

Poetry is personal,
poetry is fun,
poetry's exciting
for everyone!

Pocket Poetry Mini-Books was created for just that reason. These twelve little poetry collections give children a chance to read together, read alone, or take poetry home in a back pocket to share with families—and read again and again! Children will get to make, fold, color and personalize their very own mini-books—all while building reading skills.

These little anthologies are pocket-sized literacy-builders—they'll strengthen oral language and reading skills! Children will:

- Read and listen to repetitive, rhyming text.

- Be encouraged to read the poems over and over, building reading fluency.

- Provide a line or two at the end of each book, making each anthology an interactive literacy experience.

- Experience different genres of poetry— haiku, rhyming poems, concrete (visual) poems, nursery rhymes and chants, and so on.

- Enjoy poetry on a variety of popular themes: Colors, animals, holidays, birthdays, transportation, weather and the seasons, 100th day of school, bugs, and more!

Kindergartners and first graders will be able to listen to the poems and take them home to read with their families.

Second graders can be challenged to read them on their own or follow along as you read.

Third graders can read the poems aloud independently.

Using the Mini-Books

Once the mini-books have been assembled, you can read and enjoy them in many ways:

- Read the poems aloud as children follow along.
- Have children color the illustrations.
- Have individual children reread the poetry aloud to the class.
- Let children pair up and take turns reading to each other.
- Act out the poems, or read them in "two voices," alternating lines or verses.
- Write a poem on pocket chart strips, read it aloud, and explore its rhymes and sound patterns.
- Send poems home for children to enjoy with their families.

There are many options for picking the order in which you use the books. You might:

- Go in order. The mini-books are arranged in seasonal order, with spooky poems near the beginning for Halloween, number poems for the 100th day of school in winter, bugs in spring, and end-of-school poems at the end.
- Pick a mini-book that matches your current theme.
- Use the mini-books for reading a poem a day, or a poem a week.
- Consider cross-curricular connections. Use the number poems and some of the birthday poems in conjunction with math. The bug poems and the weather poems work well with the science curriculum, and poems on transportation might fit into your social studies themes.

Assembling the Mini-Books

It is best to assemble the books together as a class. You might assemble one yourself before walking children through the steps so that they can see the finished product.

For all the books:

1. Copy the pages for books on standard 8 1/2-inch by 11-inch paper, making the pages double-sided.

2. Cut along the solid lines and fold along the dashed lines.

3. Place the pages in order and staple along the spine.

Making the Mini-Books

Page 9

A Rainbow of Color
This little treasury of color poems will brighten children's days.

- Invite children to color the illustrations according to the clues in the poems.
- Invite children to write their own poem about painting a fall, winter, or spring day. To jump-start their poems, brainstorm colors for each season and give examples of first lines ("Use red to paint the crunchy maple leaves").

Page 13

Tickle Your Silly Bone
Poems can be silly!

- Ask children what makes them laugh—a tickle, a joke, a funny movie, something silly their dog does?
- For another silly time, have children write and illustrate their own versions of "Edible" on page 5.
- When all the poems have been read, you can vote on the silliest poem in the mini-book and make a graph showing the results.

Page 19

The Little Book of Big Animals
A collection of poems on a favorite theme.

- Have children brainstorm a list of animals that are particularly big, tall, or long. Then walk through the mini-book together and see which ones are included.
- Children can act out a poem, "The Lion and the Mouse" (page 10).
- Younger children can try to find the largest and smallest animals in the book (dinosaur and flea).

Page 23

Something Spooky
This mini-anthology of Halloween poetry has been carefully chosen for the primary classroom—scary, but not *too* scary!

- The poem "Halloween Night" (page 5) lends itself well to a reading in two voices. Split the class into two groups and have each group read every two lines, or every other line. Then everyone recites the last two lines together!
- For the poem "Trick-or-Treating" (page 7), let children search for all the rhyming words—they'll find a word at the end of every line!

Tried & True Rhymes
This mini-book of nursery rhymes and chants includes many old favorites.

Page 25

- In the second rhyme, children might count how many times the word "crooked" appears in the poem (8 times, counting the title).

- After sharing the tongue twisters on page 4, you might invite children to pick a consonant and write their own to share with the class.

- On page 2, children may be surprised to find that "Twinkle, Twinkle, Little Star" has a second verse!

Happy Birthday
This little collection of birthday poems makes a great in-class birthday celebration activity.

Page 27

- Enjoy some math challenges. When you get to "Twenty Days Till Pam's Birthday" (page 3), let children count to 20 by ones, twos, fives, as Pam does in the poem.

- Have children complete the back page.

Transportation
You might share this collection before a vacation, or anytime when students plan to travel with their families. Suggest that they take it with them on their journey!

Page 29

- Invite children to find all the pairs of rhyming words in "On the School Bus" (page 3).

A Tiny Book About Weather and the Seasons
Children will delight in this teeny-tiny book of season and weather poems.

Page 35

- Many of the poems are haiku, and children are given a chance to write and illustrate their own haiku about weather on page 15. Children can also do some "poetic detective work" to figure out which of the poems fit the 5-syllable, 7-syllable, 5-syllable pattern of traditional haiku.

- You can point out that the haiku on page 11 is a translation of the famous Japanese poet Basho, who lived 300 years ago. He traveled around Japan in all kinds of weather, writing haiku as he went.

- The concrete poem on page 4 represents a flock of geese flying south in a V-formation.

Page 37

The 100th Day of School

The number poems in this mini-book are tailor-made for the 100th Day of School—a day to celebrate numbers!

◎ Subtraction is the focus of "How Many Barks" (page 3), in which children can figure out how many more barks Poochie gets than Georgette.

◎ In "Two, Four, Six, Eight, Ten" (page 4), skip counting is the focus.

◎ After reading the traditional rhyme "Chook-Chook-Chook" (page 6), challenge children to find different addends that add up to ten (e.g. 6 + 4, 7 + 3)!

◎ Children can find all the numbers around them at school after reading "Numbers at School" (page 7).

Page 43

The Big Book of Little Bugs

Bugs may be little, but there's so much to say about them, they have a book of their own!

◎ You can use "Thumbprint Bugs" (page 8) as a springboard for children to create their own thumbprint bugs using an inkpad. They can make beetles, spiders, and ladybugs using a thumb, or caterpillars and ants using multiple prints.

◎ Integrate science by discussing the number of legs on insects (6) and spiders (8).

◎ On the last page of the mini-book, invite children to pick a favorite bug and write a poem in which they imagine what it would be like to be that bug.

Page 49

Guess-Me Riddles

"Guess-Me Riddles" is a completely interactive mini-book.

◎ On the last page, children are challenged to make up their own riddles, with three clues and an answer. Children's original riddles can be shared with a classmate or the whole class!

Page 53

End of School Poems

As the end of school is approaching, children have a wide range of feelings that are reflected in the poems in this mini-book.

◎ Look at the calendar to see where June falls in the year and how many months go by in the summer before it's fall again.

◎ After reading the poems in the mini-book, you can reproduce a version of the first poem, with blanks for children to fill in their different feelings.

Page 61

Make Your Own!

Children can write and illustrate their own collection on any theme!

Green Grasshopper

A grasshopper hides
   in the green spring grass.
      She knows she blends right in.

You see her when she takes a **hop**
   and shows you where
      she's been.

She disappears
   into the grass
      Until she **hops** again.

Don't try to catch her
   just give up,
      cuz she will always win!

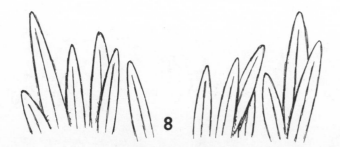

A Rainbow of Color

_____

(name)

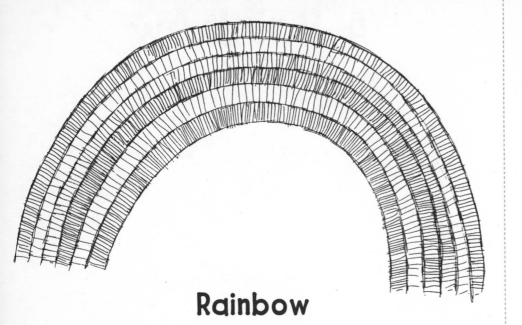

Rainbow

Pink and purple,
      green and blue;
            yellow,
                  orange,
                        crimson, too.

A wash of colors arcs the sky;
      a pot of gold
            awaits nearby.

—*Marisa Montes*

2

Red and Orange Leaves

We leap in a pile
of orange and red.
Crunch, crunch, crackle, scrunch.
We throw the leaves above our heads
in a bright and wild bunch.

7

Picnic Blue

blue lake
blue skies
bluejean shorts
blueberry pies
shoo away ants
and bumblebees
and blue-bottle flies
on the chicken, please!

4

Mixing Colors

Sunflower yellow
 and ocean blue
   make the green of a frog
   in the middle of May.

Ocean blue
 and sunset red
   make the purple in a bright bouquet.

Sunset red
 and sunflower yellow
   make pumpkin orange on Halloween day!

5

Painting a Summer Day

use breezy blue
and fluffy white
use deep, warm yellow
use clear, use bright

use open windows
use cats asleep
use leafy shadows on concrete

use splashes, sprinkles, climbing trees
strawberries, melons, fat green peas

but never, *ever* use plain gray
to paint a lovely summer day.

—Kris Aro McLeod

6

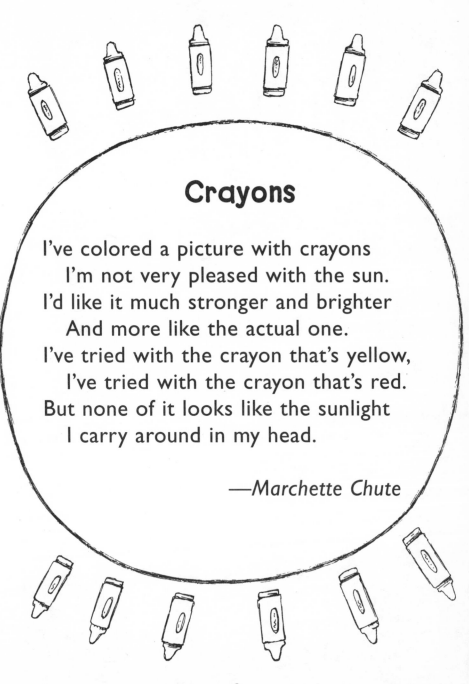

Crayons

I've colored a picture with crayons
   I'm not very pleased with the sun.
I'd like it much stronger and brighter
   And more like the actual one.
I've tried with the crayon that's yellow,
   I've tried with the crayon that's red.
But none of it looks like the sunlight
   I carry around in my head.

—*Marchette Chute*

3

Write your own
silly story or
joke here:

_____

_____

_____

_____

_____

_____

_____

12

Tickle Your Silly Bone

1

This silly little collection
of poems belongs to

_____

Two Kinds of Mice

The little gray mouse
had a letter to write
to send as a morning e-mail.
He said to the "mouse"
on the purple mouse pad,
"Hey, you've got a very long tail!"

What else would the gray mouse
say to the computer mouse?

_____

_____

_____

The Speedy Snail

The snail got awfully tired
of his slow and steady pace.
He bought himself a skateboard
and off the snail raced!

He whizzed on by the ostrich.
He whooshed on past the yak.

He just kept right on going
and he never came back.

A Laugh, A Giggle

a laugh,
a giggle,
a "ha, ha, ha,"
a snicker,
a snort,
and a big guffaw
all start with a smile
that lights up your face
and soon you're laughing
all over the place!

Tickles

Tickle your ribs, your chin, your toes.
Tickle your arms with a feather, too.
Tell me—can you tickle you?
Does tickling take one?
    Or does tickling take two?

Everyone knows you can't tickle you—
that in order to wriggle and wiggle,
you need a friend to give you a tickle
that makes you laugh and
    gets you to giggle!

4

Rhinocerecess

On the playground rhinos chase,
In a wild rhinocerace.
Up the ropes and down the slides,
Going for rhinocerides.

In a puddle rhinos stomp,
Having a rhinoceromp.
Muddy rhinos wade in pools,
Breaking the rhinocerules.

Recess ends and rhinos go,
In a neat rhinocerow,
Back to class, where they are quick
To learn rhinocerithmetic.

—Leslie Danford Perkins

9

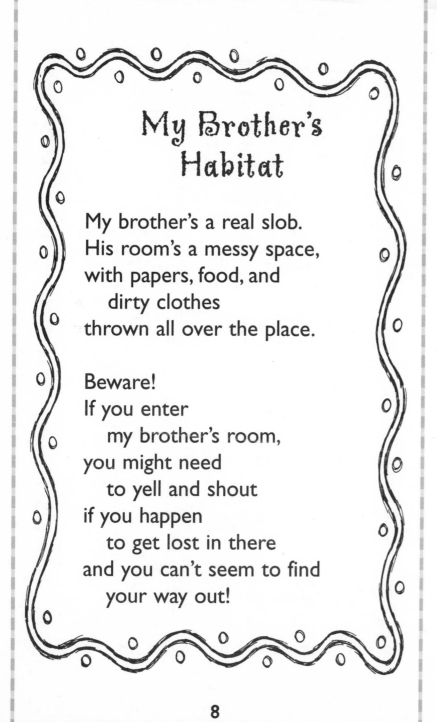

My Brother's Habitat

My brother's a real slob.
His room's a messy space,
with papers, food, and
  dirty clothes
thrown all over the place.

Beware!
If you enter
  my brother's room,
you might need
  to yell and shout
if you happen
  to get lost in there
and you can't seem to find
  your way out!

Edible

My shirt is red tomato soup.
My pockets are green peas.

My bluejeans are grape popsicles.
My socks are cottage cheese.

I have vanilla ice cream shoes
with limp spaghetti bows.

I wish I could eat everything,
but then I'd have no clothes!

—Jacqueline Sweeney

Toast and Potatoes

Rye toast,
white toast,
wheat toast, too.
I eat my toast with eggs and juice,
and so does my kangaroo.

Boiled potatoes,
Mashed potatoes
A baked potato or two.
I eat french fries with ketchup on top,
and so does my cockatoo!

I Speak English

I speak English.
My cat speaks catlish.
My mouse speaks mouselish.
My rat speaks ratlish.

My bird speaks birdlish.
My dog speaks doglish.
My duck speaks ducklish.
My frog speaks froglish.

What does my hippopotamus speak?

The End

Sailing With Whales

Sailing along in the morning wind
my father and I rode out to sea.
The gulls around us circled and cried,
around and around my father and me.
We were the only ones in sight
except for the whales and the salty foam.
We watched the whales for hours and hours
before we had to head back home.

—Sandra Liatsos

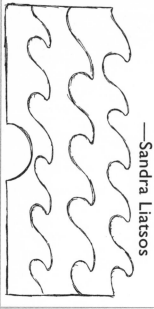

The Little Book of Big Animals

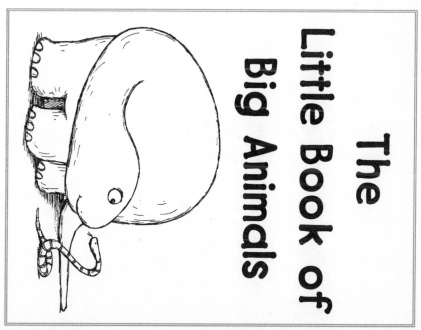

Your turn!

Write a poem about having a big animal for a pet.

If I Had a _____

If I had a _____
for a pet,
If I had a _____
for a pet,
I might get a _____ for a pet,
but I don't have one yet.

15

11

**This little book
of animal poems
belongs to**

_____

2

Two Hippos

There once was a hippo named Ty
who always felt terribly shy.
He swam near the bottom
where no one could spot him
and all you could see was his eye.

There once was a hippo named Fay
who always wanted to play.
She swam near the top
where she'd flip and she'd flop
till she'd splashed all the water away.

6

The BIG Mouse

A mouse sitting
next to a tiny flea,
looks big as a bear
and tall as a tree.

So mice can be
big or small,
you see,
depending on who
you happen to be.

The Lion and
the Mouse

One day a lion caught a mouse
who wiggled and struggled and tried
to shout.
"If you let me go," said the tiny mouse,
"someday I promise to help you out."

When the lion was caught
in a hunter's trap, the lion roared,
"OH, NO! OH, NO!"

But the mouse came back
and chewed the rope
and let that grateful lion go.

The Autograph
of a Giraffe

The autograph of a giraffe
is a very hard thing to get.
You've got to grab
her great, long neck
and climb to the top.
(You're not done yet!)

If she agrees,
then hold your hat,
for sliding back down
is your very best bet.

The Dinosaur King

The fiercest of the dinosaurs
had strong back legs and feet.
It used a mouth of very sharp teeth
to tear and eat its meat.
Its size, its face, its actions,
looked like movie special-effects.
the mighty king of dinosaurs—
TYRANNOSAURUS REX.

The Ostrich

Eight feet tall,
Eyes so small,
Neck quite long and rubbery.
Feathered body,
Speedy legs,
The ostrich is so loverly.

Elephant

An elephant's trunk is a useful tool
For squirting water to keep him cool,
For lifting up logs, or testing the trail,
Or holding hands with his mother's tail,
For sucking up peanuts or hugging
up hay,
Or feeding himself in an elephant's
way.

But why is it called a TRUNK? Who
knows?
When it isn't packed for carrying
clothes!

—Joy N. Hulme

Anaconda

As a thirty-foot snake,
I'm the longest around.
I swim in the rivers
and don't make a sound.

I'm a rainforest dweller,
and that's where I roam.
So no need to worry—
I'm not near your home!

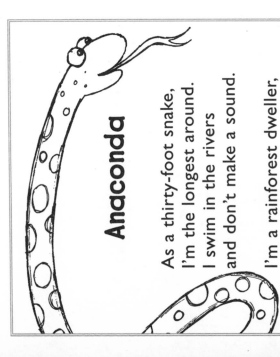

Little Monster's Lullaby

Now, boos and cackles, screeches, wails,
Most children find alarming,
But little monsters tucked in bed
Find it extremely charming.

A ghostie's groan, a mummy's moan.
Some loud and spooky screams,
Help baby monsters tucked in tight
To have the sweetest dreams.

—Robert Scotellaro

8

Something Spooky

1

Inside the Pumpkin

I carved around the pumpkin top,
but I couldn't pull it off.
I tugged and pulled with all my might,
and then I heard a cough!

I got another pumpkin
and I put the first outside—
an angry, little troll just might
be living right inside!

6

On Halloween

We mask our faces
and wear strange hats
and moan like witches
and screech like cats
and jump like goblins
and thump like elves
and almost manage
to scare ourselves.

—Aileen Fisher

3

Hey, Bat

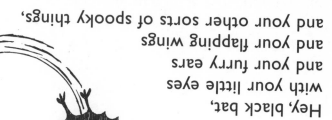

Hey, black bat,
with your little eyes
and your furry ears
and your flapping wings
and your other sorts of spooky things,
Stay up there in the moonlit sky.
Don't bother me! Just fly on by!

4

Halloween Night

Howling wind
spiders spin
skeletons creak
kids shriek

Hissing cats
flapping bats
owls hoot
spirits spook

We all scream,
"It's Halloween!"
—Joan Cottle

5

I'm a Ghost

I'm a mostly-ghostly ghost
On this eerie, feary night,
As I float around the town
Looking mostly-ghostly white.

You will quake and shake with fear
When you know a ghost is near.
If you give me tasty treats,
I'll go haunt on other streets.
—Joy N. Hulme

2

Trick-or-Treating

Pumpkin candles spit and spark.
Backyard dogs howl and bark.
A jet black cat makes an arc.
Wispy ghosts run through the park.

Trick-or-treating in the dark,
I stay beside my brother Mark!

7

The End

8

Tried
& True
Rhymes

1

Tongue Twisters

She sells sea shells
by the sea shore.

Fuzzy Wuzzy was a bear.
Fuzzy Wuzzy had no hair.
Fuzzy Wuzzy wasn't very
fuzzy, was he?

If Peter Piper picked a
peck of pickled peppers,
Where is the peck of
pickled peppers
Peter Piper picked?

How much wood would
a woodchuck chuck
if a woodchuck would
chuck wood?

4

Poems for Pals

There are gold ships,
There are silver ships,
But there's no ship
Like friendship.

Make new friends
but keep the old.
One is silver
and the other gold.

U R 2 good
2 B
4 got 10.

5

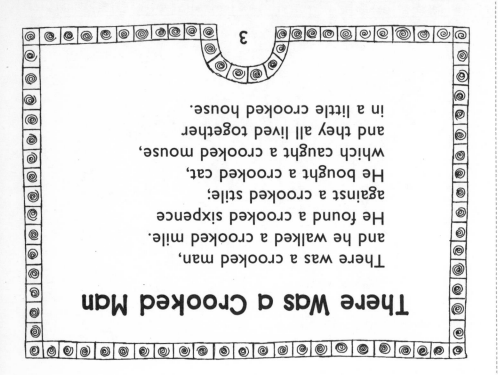

There Was a Crooked Man

There was a crooked man,
and he walked a crooked mile.
He found a crooked sixpence
against a crooked stile;
He bought a crooked cat,
which caught a crooked mouse,
and they all lived together
in a little crooked house.

3

Hey Diddle Diddle

Hey diddle, diddle,
The cat and the fiddle.
The cow jumped over the moon.
The little dog laughed
To see such sport,
And the dish ran away with the spoon.

6

Write your own tongue twister.

_____

_____

_____

_____

7

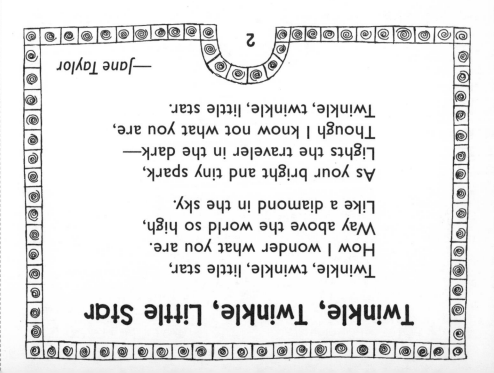

Twinkle, Twinkle, Little Star

Twinkle, twinkle, little star,
How I wonder what you are.
Way above the world so high,
Like a diamond in the sky.
As your bright and tiny spark,
Lights the traveler in the dark—
Though I know not what you are,
Twinkle, twinkle, little star.

—Jane Taylor

2

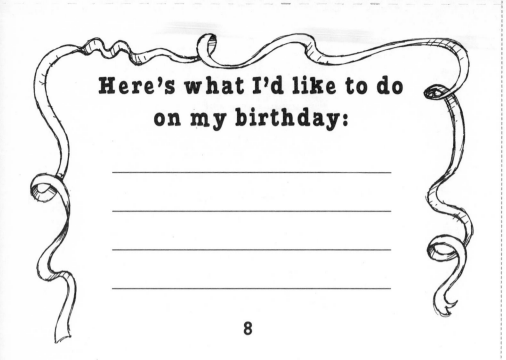

Here's what I'd like to do on my birthday:

_____

_____

_____

_____

8

Happy Birthday

This birthday book belongs to

_____

whose birthday is

_____

1

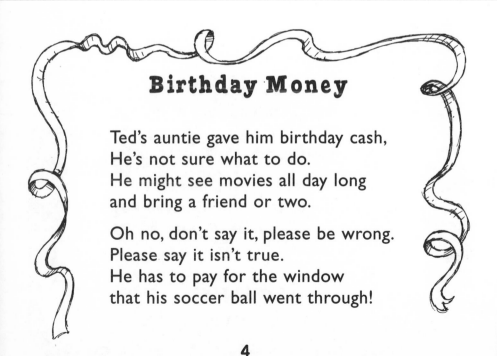

Birthday Money

Ted's auntie gave him birthday cash,
He's not sure what to do.
He might see movies all day long
and bring a friend or two.

Oh no, don't say it, please be wrong.
Please say it isn't true.
He has to pay for the window
that his soccer ball went through!

4

Birthday Party Invitations

When planning my party,
my list grew and grew.
I really don't know what to do.

I want to have Tommy
and Cindy and Sue,
and Jimmy, to name just a few.

I hope Mom agrees
that one party won't do—
that this year I'll just have to have two!

5

Twenty Days Till Pam's Birthday

Pam's birthday's coming very soon,
and Pam can hardly wait.
She checks her mother's calendar
to find the special date.
She counts the days by twos and fives.
She counts in many ways.
But it doesn't matter how she counts,
it's always twenty days!

Stretching Out My Birthday

On Wednesday,
I brought some cupcakes
to share with kids at school.
On Friday, all my relatives
brought presents that were cool.
I had my party Saturday
with all my favorite friends.
I'd like to stretch it out
so that my birthday never ends.

Which Cake?

Vanilla, lemon, or chocolate cake?
Regular frosting or coconut flakes?
A cake to freeze, or one to bake?
What flavor of ice cream should I take?
I'm not sure what my dad should make
for my extra-special birthday cake.
There's really no way to make a mistake,
but which would you choose,
for goodness sake!

—Robert Scotellaro

My Little Brother's Birthday

My little brother's birthday
Was a very big event.
The postman nearly strained his back
With presents that were sent.
My brother got a lot of stuff
Too numerous for namin'.
But all he ever played with were
The boxes that they came in.

Transportation:
Getting from
Here to There

This little book
of traveling poems
belongs to:

_____

2

Now write your own poem!
Imagine you are in a big, noisy city at night.
Use the sounds in the box to finish the poem:

honk	toot	screech
vroom	crash	

Sound Around Town

_____, _____, _____,

Beep, beep, beep!

_____, _____, _____,

I can't sleep!

11

Traveling Food

In flies the meat
on a zooming jet.
In chug the beans
on a railroad train.
In race the peas
on a chestnut horse.
We're feeding
the baby lunch,
of course.

On the School Bus

Wheels a-rolling 'neath the bus
down the road you carry us
past the trees of brown and gold
past the store where toys are sold
past the playground where we play
past the zoo where tigers stay,
over the bridge and up the hill
wheels a-rolling, rolling still
while we joke and smile and fool
riding all the way to school.

—*Sandra Liatsos*

City Traffic

Beep, honk, step on the brake.
City traffic makes us wait.

Taxis dodging here and there.
Cars and vans are everywhere.

Blinking stoplights flash and glow.
City traffic's stop and go.

Buses pick up girls and boys.
Trucks look like they're giant toys.

All this traffic's really cool,
but it makes us late for school!

Visiting Grandma

We pile in the car
and drive really far.
We travel by plane
and ride on a bus.
We get picked up
in a pickup truck
that goes to the barn
on grandma's farm,
and once we're there,
to get somewhere—
we ride her horses everywhere!

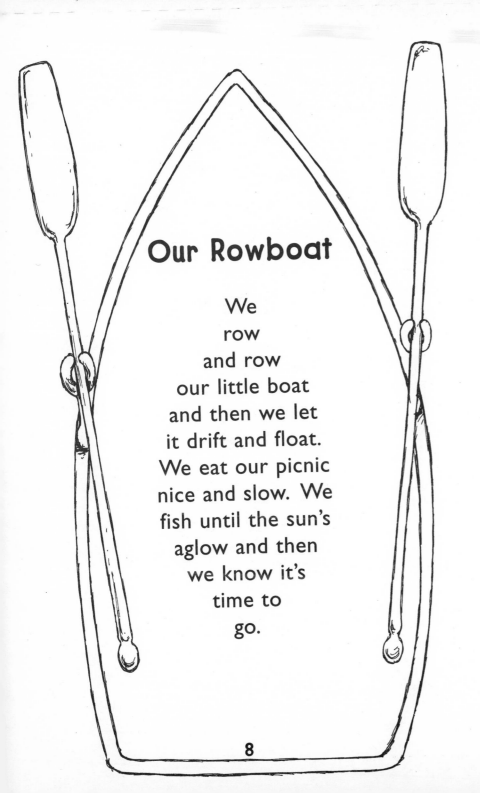

Our Rowboat

We
row
and row
our little boat
and then we let
it drift and float.
We eat our picnic
nice and slow. We
fish until the sun's
aglow and then
we know it's
time to
go.

8

I'd Like to Fly

I'd like to be a pilot
who flies to Kenya or to Spain.
Or maybe I'd take my friends aboard
my small, two-seater plane.

Or better yet, I'd blast to the Moon
and look back at the world.
A man has already walked up there,
but I'd be the very first girl!

5

Animal Transportation

The grasshopper has his legs to hop.
The monkey swings from tree to tree.
The green snake slithers.
The jellyfish pumps.
The penguin waddles near the ice-cold sea.
And guess who walks and skips and runs—
Children just like you and me!

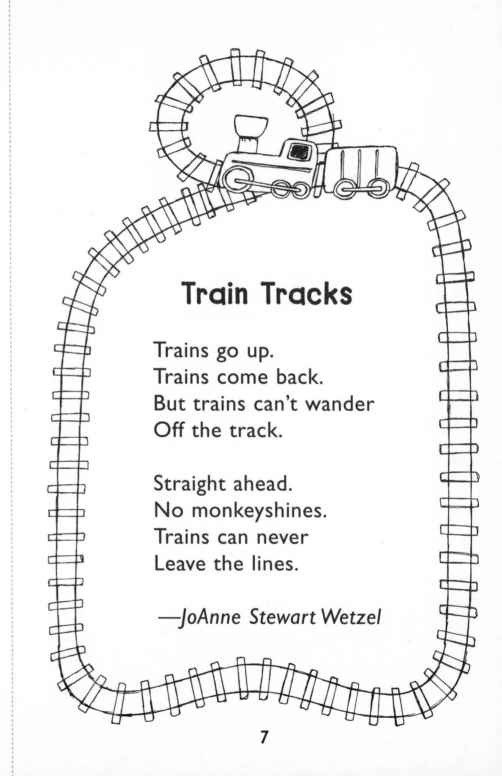

Train Tracks

Trains go up.
Trains come back.
But trains can't wander
Off the track.

Straight ahead.
No monkeyshines.
Trains can never
Leave the lines.

—JoAnne Stewart Wetzel

16

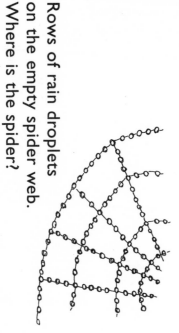

Thunder! Bright lightning!
Alone in my room, I dive
under the covers.

14

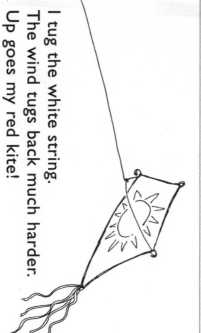

I tug the white string.
The wind tugs back much harder.
Up goes my red kite!

12

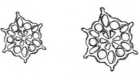

Rows of rain droplets
on the empty spider web.
Where is the spider?

10

A Tiny Book
About Weather
and the Seasons

1

Fall Haiku

No more games of chase
for the squirrels in my backyard—
too many fall chores!

3

Autographing Winter

I blow upon
the windowpane
and with my finger
write my name.
— *Anita Wintz*

5

Ice Bird

I skate like a bird
swooping and gliding on ice
no one can catch me
—*Monica Kulling*

7

Pick your favorite season. Use three lines to describe something you see, hear, taste, touch, or smell in that season.

_____

_____

_____

15

SUMMER

June is a bumble
of one small bee.

June is a hug
from the sunshine
to me.

—*Sarah Wilson*

13

A quiet old pond
In jumps a frog
The sound of the splash!

—*Bashō*

11

Rain Cloud

Rain spills like pennies
from bulging piggy bank clouds
clinking on concrete

—*Katie McAllaster Weaver*

9

Wind

When mischievous wind
sneaks up on crisp autumn leaves—
they scuttle like crabs

—*Liza Charlesworth*

2

The
geese
know
when
it's time
to fly.
their
good-byes.
honking
them
I hear

4

Sledding

Fresh winter snowfall—
whooshing down the steep hillside,
covered with snowdust.

6

Winter Sweetness

This little house is sugar.
Its roof with snow is piled,
And from its tiny window
Peeps a maple-sugar child.

—*Langston Hughes*

8

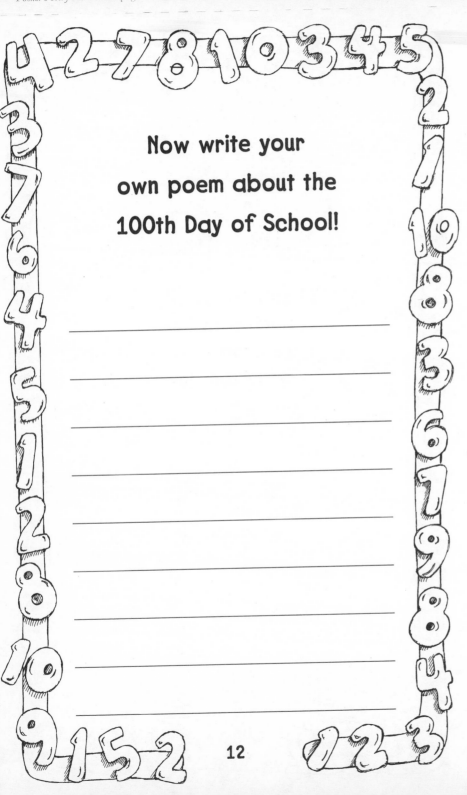

Now write your
own poem about the
100th Day of School!

_____

_____

_____

_____

_____

_____

12

The
100th
Day
of
School

1

Baby Teeth

I've lost teeth,
and so have you.
The spaces in front,
make it hard to chew.

You've lost four
and I've lost two.
That's six in all,
and we're not even
through!

2

One, Two

One, two,
   buckle my shoe.
Three, four,
   close the door.
Five, six,
   pick up sticks.
Seven, eight,
   close the gate.
Nine, ten,
   a big fat hen!

11

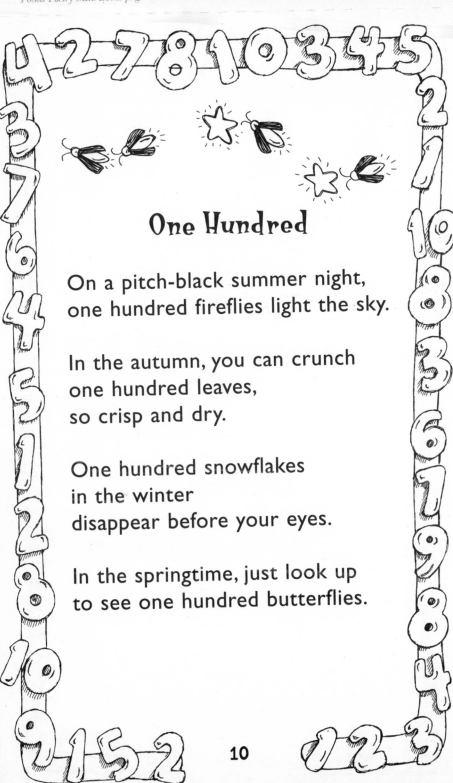

One Hundred

On a pitch-black summer night,
one hundred fireflies light the sky.

In the autumn, you can crunch
one hundred leaves,
so crisp and dry.

One hundred snowflakes
in the winter
disappear before your eyes.

In the springtime, just look up
to see one hundred butterflies.

10

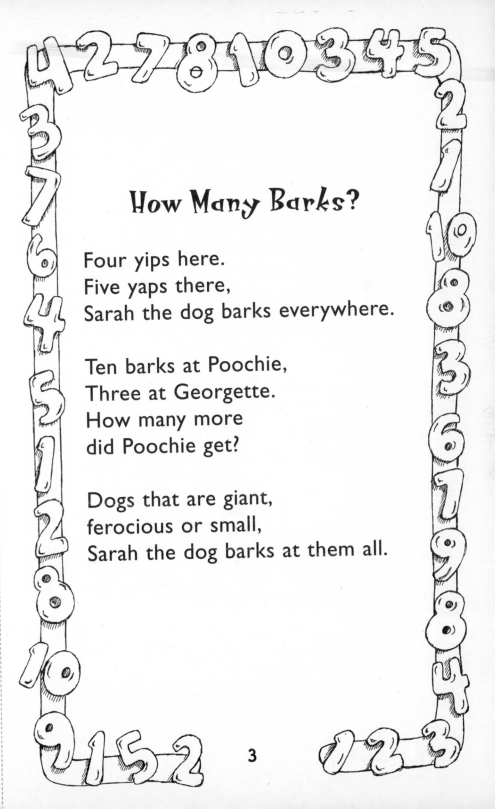

How Many Barks?

Four yips here.
Five yaps there,
Sarah the dog barks everywhere.

Ten barks at Poochie,
Three at Georgette.
How many more
did Poochie get?

Dogs that are giant,
ferocious or small,
Sarah the dog barks at them all.

3

Two, Four, Six, Eight, Ten

Two eyes on one cat,
Four eyes on two.
Six eyes on three cats—
staring at you.

Eight eyes on four cats,
Ten eyes on five.
Ten eyes in the dark—
glowing and alive!

4

The Hundredth Day

I brought 100 slippery snails
but I forgot to cover my pail!

One hundred snails,
one hundred trails!

Around the counter, up the walls,
across the carpet, down the halls!

It just might take 100 days.
to find those snails that got away.

—Kris Aro McLeod

9

My Cousin Trix

I'm older than my cousin Trix.
When she was five, I was six.
When Trix is twelve,
or twenty-four,
I'll always be
just one year more.

When Trixie's age is ninety-nine,
just stop and think,
and then guess mine!

8

One Potato

One potato, two potato
three potato, four
five potato, six potato
seven potato, MORE!

5

Chook-Chook-Chook

Chook, chook,
chook-chook-chook.
Good Morning,
Mrs. Hen.
How many chickens
have you got?
Madam, I've got ten.

Four of them
Are yellow,
And four of them
Are brown,
And two of them
Are speckled red—
The nicest in the town!

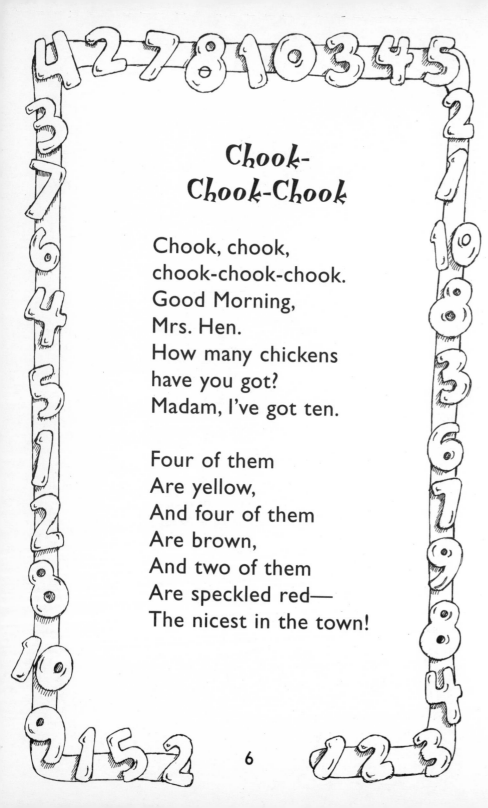

6

Numbers at School

14 girls in our classroom,
53 nuts in the counting jar,
75 kids on the playground,
Just look at all the numbers
there are!

26 bikes in the bike rack,
14 coats in the lost and found,
225 kids in our school,
Find all the numbers!
Look around!

7

The Big Book of Little Bugs

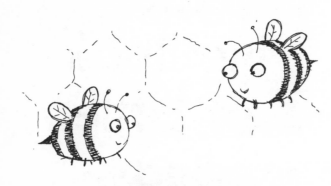

This buggy book belongs to:

_____

2

Your Turn

Pick a bug. Write its name in each of the short blanks. On the longer blanks, imagine what it would be like to be that bug.

A _____

If I were a _____,

I'd _____.

If I were a _____,

I'd _____.

If I were a _____,

I'd _____.

But if I were a _____,

then I wouldn't be me!

11

Tell a butterfly
your secrets,
and she will whisper them
into the ear of every
curious flower.

—Caryn Yacowitz

My Cocoon

If I began as a butterfly's egg,
I'd hatch right out and try out my legs.

I'd grow and grow till the time was right,
Then I'd spin a cocoon so cozy and tight.

I'd rest like a baby tucked into bed,
and dreams of wings would fill my head.

Then I'd wake and stretch out toward the light
and my wings would be an amazing sight!

Respect

Do ants have feelings just like me?
Are beetles ever sad?
Do bugs feel bad when kids say, "yuck"?
Do butterflies feel glad?

Do spiders get upset inside
when their spider webs are wrecked?
Would all the millions of little bugs
just like to get respect?

Would You Like?

(Sing to the tune of "Do Your Ears Hang Low?")

If the bumblebees
put their stingers all away,
would you like to live
in a beehive for a day?
If the queen came back
to her growing honeycomb,
we could all run home!

Bugs Playing Tricks

Is that a little stick I see?
But wait, is it a trick?
That's not a broken twig at all
but a slender walkingstick.

If that a speckled leaf I see?
But wait, it just flew off.
That's not a falling leaf at all,
but a polka-dotted moth.

Roly-Poly Bug

Hey, roly-poly
potato bug,
Why do you act so shy?
When I pick you up,
you give yourself a hug,
and roll in a ball
so cozy and snug!

Thumbprint Bugs

I make a dark black thumbprint bug,
and draw eight legs that make it wider.
I make another print in red and draw in dots.
Now this bug's much brighter.
Can you guess the bugs I made?
A thumbprint ladybug and spider!

Fireflies

Winking, blinking,
winking, blinking,
See that little light.
Now it's here,
Now it's there,
Now it's out of sight.
Winking, blinking,
winking, blinking,
Fireflies at night.

Stars With Wings

Sometimes it seems
like all the stars
have fallen
from the skies,
but when I see
the stars have wings
I know they're fireflies.

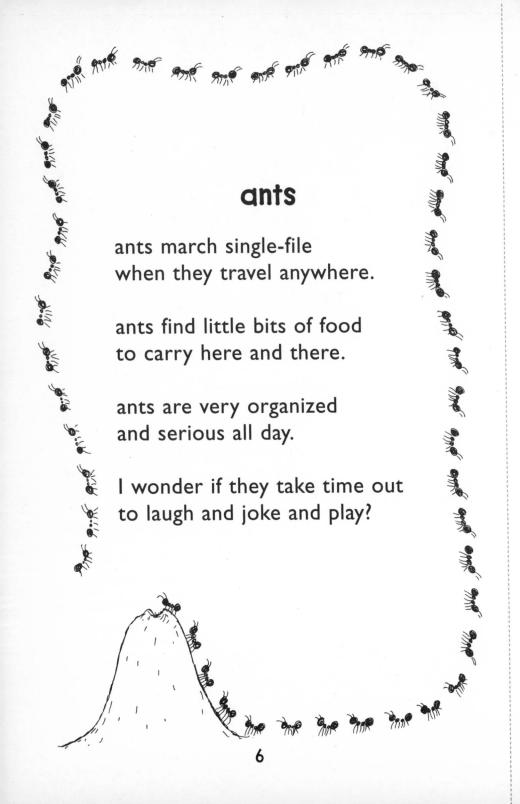

ants

ants march single-file
when they travel anywhere.

ants find little bits of food
to carry here and there.

ants are very organized
and serious all day.

I wonder if they take time out
to laugh and joke and play?

Spider

I spy a silent spider
hanging from a thread.

I hope the spider spies this fly
buzzing round my head.

—Lawrence Schimel

Spider Web

Walking through a spider web
is a very itchy, twitchy thing—
the spider's mad
and you're not glad
that spider thread
and maybe flies
and other things that spiders chew
are draped and stuck
all over you.

6

7

Your turn!

Write your own riddle about a food. Write 3 clues.

I _____

I _____

I _____

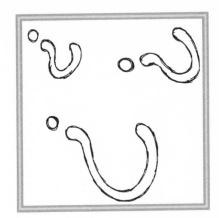

What am I?

Answer: _____

14

16

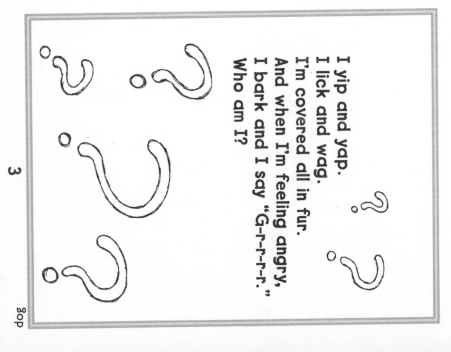

I yip and yap.
I lick and wag.
I'm covered all in fur.
And when I'm feeling angry,
I bark and I say "G-r-r-r-r."
Who am I?

3

Guess-Me Riddles

1

Now write another riddle
about anything you like.

I _____

I _____

I _____

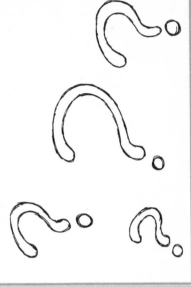

What am I?

Answer: _____

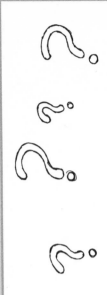

You wrap me round your finger
and then you let me go.
I spin as I go up and down.
You call me your...

This little book
of riddles
belongs to

_____

Slither, slither.
Hiss-s-s, hiss-s-s,
Without any legs I move like
This-s-s, this-s-s.
Who am I?

—Stephanie Calmenson

You fly me
in the wind in spring.
I wave my tail.
You hold my string.
What am I?

10

kite

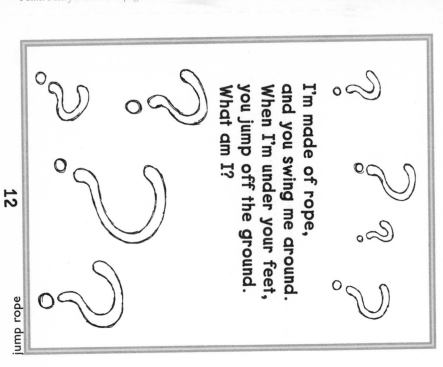

I'm made of rope,
and you swing me around.
When I'm under your feet,
you jump off the ground.
What am I?

12

jump rope

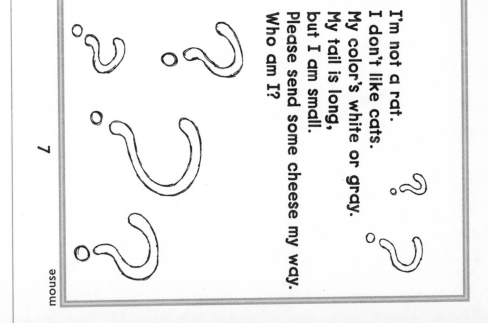

I'm not a rat.
I don't like cats.
My color's white or gray.
My tail is long,
but I am small.
Please send some cheese my way.
Who am I?

7

mouse

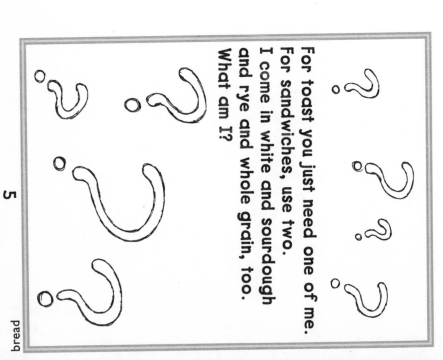

For toast you just need one of me.
For sandwiches, use two.
I come in white and sourdough
and rye and whole grain, too.
What am I?

5

bread

balloon

BLOW
and I'll grow.
STOP
or I'll pop.
TIE
or I'll fly.
What
am
I?

—Anita Wintz

6

apple

You pick me off an autumn tree
I grow there way up high.
You mash me into applesauce
or put me in a pie.
Which fruit am I?

11

fish

I swim in water all day long.
You feed me little flakes.
If I were wild and not a pet,
I'd live in streams and lakes.
Who am I?

8

ice cream

I'm cold and creamy.
I'm smooth and sweet.
When it's hot outside,
I'm hard to beat.

You eat me
from a crunchy cone,
with stuff on top,
or all alone.

Hey! Quiet down!
No need to scream.
Politely ask for more...

—Kris Aro McLeod

9

Next year I'd like to:

16

End of School Poems

1

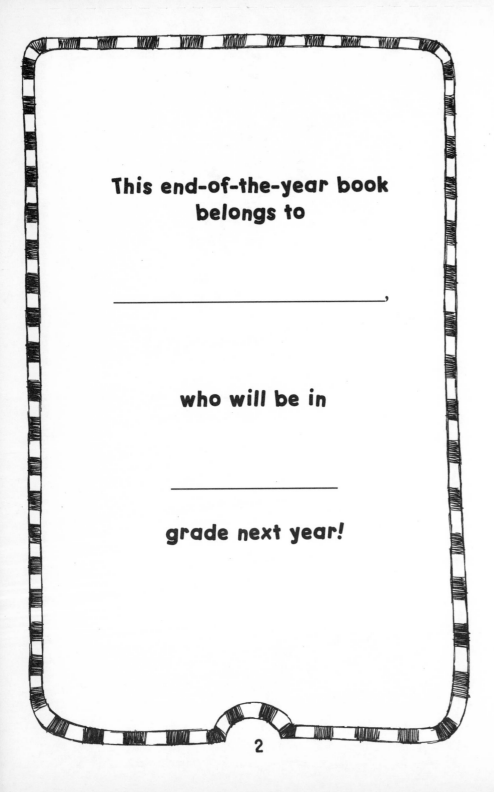

This end-of-the-year book belongs to

_____,

who will be in

_____

grade next year!

2

The best things about this year were:

_____

_____

_____

_____

_____

_____

_____

_____

15

Autographs

14

Last Days of School

I'm happy, I'm ready,
I'm silly, I'm sad.
I'm jolly, I'm jumpy,
I'm lazy, I'm glad.
I've got many feelings
'cause school's almost done.
I'll miss many things,
but I know I'll have fun!

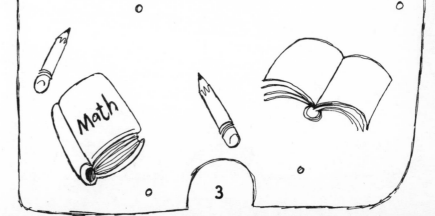

3

Beginnings and Endings

On the first day of school,
everything's new—
kids and teachers,
books and pens.

By the last day of school,
everything's cool—
you've learned lots of things
and you've made some
good friends!

4

Autographs

13

Autographs

12

In the School Room

The windows are open
and I can see
a bright red cardinal
up in a tree.
He's singing and singing
a wonderful tune
that says,
"Come outdoors!
At last it's June!"

—*Sandra Liatsos*

5

When School
Is Over

When the school year
is completed,
and we've all said
our farewells,
the bike racks will be empty
and there will be
no more bells.

The teachers will have
all gone home.
The classrooms
will be dark.
And we will all be playing
in the pool and in the park!

6

Autographs

11

Autographs

The Garbage Dump

I'm bouncing my chair with frustration
At tackling a job so grotesque.
Before I can go on vacation
I've orders to clean out my desk.

—Marcy Black

End-of-Year Party

Munch cookies and cakes.
Drink lemonade shakes.
Play party games,
and sign your names.
Sing lots of songs,
And say, "So-longs."
Then stand up and cheer
for the end of the year!

8

Good-Bye, Friends

Good-byes can make you lonely.
Good-byes can make you glad.
They often have some hugs in them.
Sometimes they're kind of sad.

Good-bye, my special school friends.
We've really had a ball.
I'll see you in the neighborhood
or back at school next fall.

9

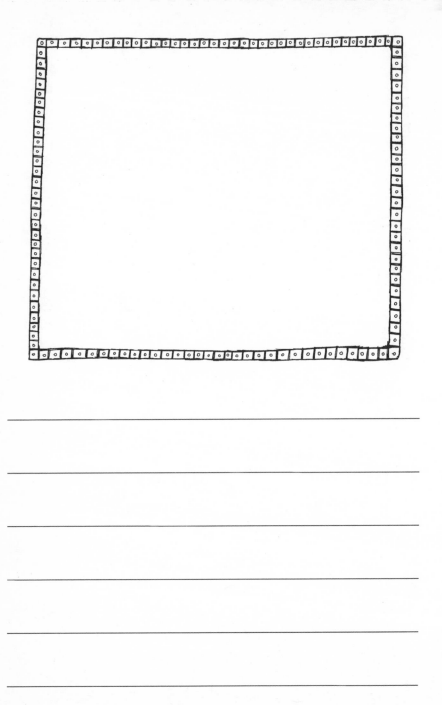

_____

_____

_____

_____

_____

_____

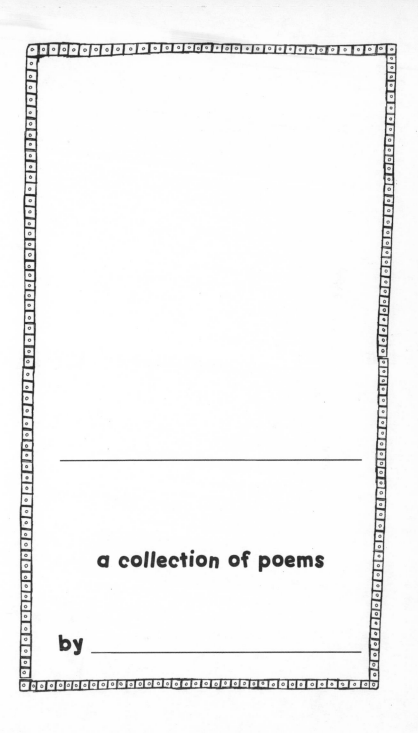

_____

a collection of poems

by _____

_____

_____

_____

_____

_____

_____

_____

_____

_____

_____

Notes

Notes